EIGHT FRAMES EIGHT

for Rob Bennett — whose great and rare knowledge insures the preservation of classical music and letters — my very best wishes —
Judith Cody
March 28 - 2003

EIGHT FRAMES EIGHT

Judith Cody

Copyright © 2002 by Judith Cody.

Library of Congress Number:		2001117363
ISBN #:	Hardcover	1-4010-1360-0
	Softcover	1-4010-1361-9

All rights reserved. No part of this book may be reproduced or transmitted in any form or by any means, electronic or mechanical, including photocopying, recording, or by any information storage and retrieval system, without permission in writing from the copyright owner.

This book was printed in the United States of America.

To order additional copies of this book, contact:
Xlibris Corporation
1-888-795-4274
www.Xlibris.com
Orders@Xlibris.com

CONTENTS

Prologue 15

PART ONE *Primary Colors*

Watching Half-Dome from Yosemite Valley 19
Entering the Singing Place 21
Moth in the Footlights 22
Blink 23
The Merchant 26
Skimming the Subconscious: After reading Gertrude
    Stein's "Tender Buttons" 28
Consider the Death of Dragons 30
Heat 31
Three Worlds Dissolve 32
Now and Then the Carpenter 33
When Dreams Emerge like Butterflies 34
After the Growing Time 35
Woman Magic 38
Watching for Tlaloc to Cool the Sun 42
Ars Longa Vita Brevis 44
Danger Dance 46

PART TWO *Perspective*

Snodgrass Survival Manuals 51
Ollej of the Mythic Warriors 52
A Minor Distraction 55
The Starmaker 56

Blue Boy on Dark Background 57
The Neon Model and the Ad Man 59
The Headhunter's Wife 61
The Justice Proclamation 63
Inspection by Daylight 64
Medical Music 65
Flycasting 66
Past. Future? 67
Women's Year Poem 70
Dark Glasses 71

PART THREE   *Lifeblood*

Looking Under Footprints 75
When the Wind Fans a Spider Web 77
Say It 78
A Smile 80
Topics over Tea 81
Once Upon A Time the Marble Statue Became
    A Real Live Man 85
Encounter 86
Odonata 88
Save the Visions 89
Loving Poem 90
Plato's Hermaphrodite 91
Lovers and Other Spies 93
Unmentioned 94
The Alison Rainbow Song 95

PART FOUR   *Soul Tears*

The Forever Diorama 103
Who Killed the Vulture While He Waited for
    the Beached Whale to Die? 105
The Printer 106

Child of the Virgins 107
The Exhumation 110
Akhenaton's Hymn to Aton 112
No Refunds, No Exchanges 113
Stillbirths 114
Biological War Needles 116
Elegy 117
The Offering 118
The Tear God 119
Woman Left on a Desert Plateau 120
The Blanket 121
Wings of Glory 126
Wrapping Gifts 127
California Drought makes TV Winter News 128
Three True Wolves 130

PART FIVE *Epilogue*

Notes and Thoughts on the Poems 133
Dedications 137

for Bunky

ACKNOWLEDGMENTS

"The Starmaker;" "Topics Over Tea . . . philosophy student;" "Ollej of the Mythic Warriors;" "Moth in the Footlights;" "The Tear God;" "The Merchant;" "Entering the Singing Place;" "Watching Half-Dome from Yosemite Valley;" "The Forever Diorama;" "Exhumation;" "Looking Under Footprints;" "Danger Dance;" "Who Killed the Vulture While He Waited for the Beached Whale to Die?;" "Ars Longa Vita Brevis;" published in *Foreground*.

"Watching for Tlaloc to Cool the Sun" won the Amelia Native American Poetry Theme Award 1993, and published by *Amelia*.

"The Merchant" won third prize, Atlantic Monthly Creative Writing Contest and published by *The Atlantic Monthly*.

"Akhenaton's Hymn to Aton;" "Snodgrass Survival Manuals;" published in *Sequoia*.

"The Merchant;" "Entering the Singing Place;" published in *Foothill Sentinel*.

"Medical Music;" published in *Stonecloud*.

"Watching Half-Dome from Yosemite Valley;" published in *Poetry Project IV*.

"Plato's Hermaphrodite;" published in *Androgyne*.

"Blink" was published as a broadside by the American Medical Electroencephalographic Association and was the keynote opening for a national meeting.

"Women's Year Poem," as a group of eight posters and broadsides in English and in Spanish was placed in the permanent collection of the *National History Museum* of the *Smithsonian Institution*, Washington, DC; permanent and touring collection of the *Women's Heritage Museum*, Palo Alto, CA, and published by *Palo Alto Times* newspaper, by Kikimora Publishing Company, by Texas Women's University, and in the *NOW Bulletin*.

"Woman Magic;" published by Kikimora Publishing Co.

"Odonata;" "Blink;" "Watching Half-Dome from Yosemite Valley;" "Who Killed the Vulture While He Waited for the Beached Whale to Die?;" "Looking Under Footprints;" "After the Growing Time;" "Entering the Singing Place;" and "When the Wind Fans a Spider Web;" were presented in formal readings of *Environment and Science Poetry* at the National Aeronautics and Space Administration, NASA; and at the San Francisco Bay National Wildlife Refuge for observance of *National Wildlife Week;* and also on *National Astronomy Day*.

Numerous poems in this collection have been read on radio stations *KKUP.FM* in Cupertino, CA; *KFJC.FM* in Los Altos, CA; and television station *Gill Cable* in San Jose, CA.

"Looking Under Footprints" was the theme poem for the GillCable TV Show called *Contemporary Poetry*, channel 11, San Jose, CA.

"Danger Dance" was part of a concert by Judith Cody at the *Sunday Afternoon Concert Series*, Palo Alto Cultural Center, sponsored by the City of Palo Alto, CA.

"Topics Over Tea . . . philosophy student" is part of a continuing poetry cycle, sections of which, "Topics Over Tea . . . one cup" and "Topics Over Tea . . . thermos" were performed (both are poetry plays) at the Santa Cruz Arts Center, Santa Cruz, CA; and at the Palo Alto Cultural Center, Palo Alto, CA.

PROLOGUE

If I should walk through the woods and step on a small snake, it would take, some experts say, one eighth of a second for the sensation of snakeness to travel from foot to brain and cause me to leap away. When you stare at the person you just fell in love with, you are also blinking many times each minute, so that there are "blank" scenes between most of the "real" scenes of that man or woman you see as unique.

This "Blink" time (the poem on page 23) is the void between episodes of our vision of our individual worlds. Yet, wonderful for us all, our brains have learned to correct this choppy picture, and all looks perfect.

Of course, "love is blind," but is this what is meant? Much of the reality we see or feel is somewhat missing; could it be that our brains fill in the blanks with the wrong stuff now and then? Yes. When a relationship ends with all the pain, the self-criticism, the sudden shock of emptiness, we know at once that we didn't understand at all. Why, why? becomes a mantra, a wound.

Our bodies have betrayed us in some strange chemically way: we instinctively know this. In the very instance of this inner knowledge, our bodies' spirit has sustained us. At the deepest level of our identities, the spirit, the cellular memories, the archetypes, are almost invincible. It is at this level that poetry attempts to answer the universe surrounding us. That is why everyone is born with the capability to do a poem, in their personal manner.

Eight Frames Eight is the velocity of the Universe entering ourselves; the waltz time of our response to love, to hate, to life.

These flickering perceptions assume an eerie cast when their sharply limited physical dimensions are understood. Take the "laws" of *perspective*, it seems natural that the lines of a road converge in the distance and that a nearby house is large, though, the house on the horizon appears tiny. Yet, if I were blindfolded and walked that same road it would always be the same width to my sensation of touch. The house in the distance would never seem small to my fingers. Is what we "see" or is what we "touch" our world's true configuration?

Earthly perceptions are like millions of fireflies glowing off and on in an immense blackness. At any instant only some are visible. It isn't possible to see them all. We must focus on only those we want to catch. If we can.

Ironically, the limits and distortions of our biological conformations lend a terrible, wonderful, mysterious quality to life. Mystery lies in the gaps between perceptions and in the deep blackness surrounding the fireflies. That which we call spirit moves invisibly among the firefly-like events of everyday life that we think of as the only world. Mystery lies in the intimate discovery of finding the lifelong poem we each will create from this knowledge.

While looking for that mystery I found the poems in this book.

PART ONE
Primary Colors

WATCHING HALF-DOME FROM YOSEMITE VALLEY

Supine, through the cradle of my thighs
I watch the sun slowly set between my legs.
It descends beneath the birth bone
disappears and forms a flaming halo through my pubic hair.

Curls are solar flares seen through the red mist.

This is my day, I have taken its last display
into a dark place where I embrace it,
grasp it firmly by its flaming tail
and watch it sprawl against the grass
beside me.

Prone, over the edge of my arms
I watch the stars outside my head,
they ascend over thought
and point white slivers at my naked back.

Cold shouts through the dark.

I am beyond cold sounds,
no white sliver will frighten me.
I have wrestled with the day
and here between my body and the ground
I press the heated red distress
like grapes.

The sun has gone into the moon cave
I lock the entrance
with a small twist of my ankles.

In the black night the day is mine
where I can probe the waning warmth
with my own flame,
and study the shape of noon,
recall the sun rise over a Half-Dome
and wrap around the afternoon
a crescent prison with my ribs.

ENTERING THE SINGING PLACE

The cat's belly sand,
foot scratched, fish scarred,
stretches, waiting
for the sea's mating call
singing octaves
above the range
of human comprehension.

The sea arches, caught
in convulsive
culmination,
at this meeting
arranged before
fishes sought the land,
before I heard
my section of the song.

MOTH IN THE FOOTLIGHTS

Like the geisha's
pale silk fans,
wings breathed
an age-old meter
against the air,
they quivered on the arcs

of an undulating course
with an inborn certainty
of each impending pulse
raising in the destined
flux and reflux,

then small with concentration
the moth circumscribed
its tremulous
life flight's passage,
a scant hand-span
above the stage.

BLINK

At eight frames per second
the Universe jerks
in spasmodic brilliancies
smashing the eye-rods.

Light.

Blink.

Light.

Cones absorb,
in minute
pigment baths
the primary,

red.

yellow.

blue.

Geometries of construction
converge in Lilliputian exits,
paths too narrow for feet,
houses tossed on the horizon,
like dice I could squeeze
in the damp of my hand.

Blink.

Sun, seeping through eyelids
casts a blood-tinged negative
Universe,
reversing itself
on arterial throbs,
spurting an image
onto the mind.

Blink.

Aberrational hues,
from the most distant
peripheries,
are focused upside down,
in a walnut-sized
jelly globe.

Blink.

The spectrum
is sucked from its star
at eight frames per second
of twitching arcs,
sieving the coronal order
into discharged flecks
stuck to a cell.

Blink.

THE MERCHANT

Bees are driven to account
for their euphoria
and dance an
animated compass.
The lilac scented girl
incites them to forage.

Hummingbirds careen into
the red columbine
dyed on her dress,
they lie in broken tufts
scuffed by her quick
varnished toes.

Fondling the fabric
of her thin retreat
she is the merchant
of her colored tent.

The sun is leaching
pigment from the cloth;
the wind is shredding
pennants from her hair.

She reveals the small bright wares,
the soft distractions
and colored flags
fading in the wind.

Closing shadows quench the hues
of the treasures
strewn about her feet
like crumpled birds.

SKIMMING THE SUBCONSCIOUS:

after reading Gertrude Stein's "Tender Buttons"

Below the crystal lake
of a day's reflections,
tonal fragments
echoed, argued
in a voice
a scratch on glass:
    "Kit's mean na tow?"

Why this moment
break the surface
this slim etching,
brittle sound?
So I answered
deftly, calmly:
    "The scene is snow."
I lied and
did not know.
Yet still I felt
it shake a fist
and heard its crafty whisper:
    "It's kean na go?"

Reflecting more
it yielded some
and
the image hung,
for a second,
clear as something,
a silvered thought,
sharply throbbing
out of reach.

CONSIDER THE DEATH OF DRAGONS

> "my wish . . . O to be a dragon"
> Marianne Moore

I agree with you, I'm a coward too,
I never sang my mangled aria
As loud as I could bear
Until my human noises drowned
The sound of other songs
So for an instant I could know
The world with me was flat
And raged with stars and dragons
And tasted like a tree.

O I'm afraid you'd hear me and believe,
Then tell me I must show you dragon's scales.

HEAT

1
The atmosphere is
thick and persistent,
palpable
by the entire edges
of the body.

2
Brightness presses
fluids from the eyes
stunning the brain stem,
squeezing the iris
into a knot.

3
Sun etches the skin
crisp and malignant,
sun,
maker of mummies.

THREE WORLDS DISSOLVE

Save me
petals
from your
flowers
I will
sail them
in my
coffee
sugar
grains will
sink my
vessels
to the
opaque
bottom.

In the
thousand
year old
sunset
a tall
mountain
shrank and
squatted
cringed in
to the
valley
as the
darkest
night en
closed it.

Plants in
sects birds
mammals
scurry
on the
icebergs
warm side
tending
efforts
to their
growing
while their
world tends
to its
melting.

NOW AND THEN THE CARPENTER

Here is
a bureau
built in
1780
by laughing
hands
that defined
this shape
I'm stuffing
full with
rag-tags
of my
goings.

A voice
is raising
its fingers
from a
paved over
grave and
I'm retching
and laughing
at the absurd
horror straining
beneath
an eight lane
expressway.

The carpenter
selected
a tree
and crafted
a perfect
door from it
that he
opened thousands
of times
till the final
time he opened
the tree when
the future fell.

WHEN DREAMS EMERGE LIKE BUTTERFLIES

I was stapled
by a pin
and my eyes
scratched the darkness
(wrapped and twisted)
tightly wound.

In the still cocoon
a single thought awoke,
a sound of fish
striking through the water
or lace tearing,
and waited
for a slit in the wrapping
with the light
stroking through.

AFTER THE GROWING TIME

The season has come when survival stops
and the cool night's blood bleeds into the sun,
when winter is near yet far behind
in memories before the growing time.

A year has returned again,

And

I know how the hind feels when she is still
though her strong hooves poise
ready to run,
for her eyes are quick with Autumn light.

The season is here when renewal starts
when the buck in the distance must challenge,
that pause suspended in auburn dawn,
then shake his awkward antlers against a heavy air.

And

I know what the hind feels when she hears
him moving among the trees,
as she watches with active eyes
for his rushing breath she stays to see
when he walks through the trembling leaves.

The year has revolved again,

Yet

The hind never knew, never knew until now,
when the earth must tilt from its sun,
that survival must wait
while beginning begins.

WOMAN MAGIC

Make woman magic
chant love thunder
let the blood
course in triplets
pulse in sixty-fourths
and freed within the ribs
feel the heart reach fortissimo.

Skin whispers
make woman magic.

The pelvis glides
like a small planet
into the great space

where the life song
caresses the throat
gathers crescendo
where the woman life
spins the world
like a small moon
around the hips.

Woman life
dance on the crest and quiver in the blood
dance to the edge of all continents
hum woman magic in every sound ever heard
paint woman magic on every image ever seen
breathe woman magic on every thing ever touched
show woman magic to every frightened eye.

The world is our satellite
our earth moon
our proud earth moon mother.

Birth belongs to woman
music birth
world birth
woman birth
self birth.

Explode
bear down
its all inside.

All births of all things
urge them out screaming
the life song.

Bring our unborn unities
at last
at last
with us in our life space.

Tomorrow is crowning.

Mind whispers
make woman magic
sing woman magic
to all woman life.

WATCHING FOR TLALOC TO COOL THE SUN

The first rain that happened
after the California drought
falls over me like a bridal veil.

Rain brushes the nape of my neck
rests against my arms
then bright as Quetzal feathers
shimmers against my feet.

Through mist caught in my lashes
I see the Sierra Madres
sprawl beyond the Rio Grande
beneath the silver skybride's hem.

Burnt Chaparral bends
above the summer-wrinkled earth
where the rain god waits with valleys
cupped to contain this luxury.

I know that gentle thunder is his laugh
as his rain bride descends
deserting the red sun
for Tlaloc's white embrace.

That quick cloud, her smile, I laugh
with Tlaloc and his bride
at this yearly ceremony
when the sun is cooled.

ARS LONGA VITA BREVIS

Who is the beautiful one
who smiled to me?

His mouth became the Buddha's
at Kamakura,

Traced into a curve and drawn
onto a Japanese scroll,

Laughing among the birds
perched on bamboo,

Until it grinned in bronze
detachment at my efforts

To think the crescent to a wing
the way the artist planned,

A gentle working of a brush
had shaped the paper

And my mind to feel a smile
emerge within the strokes,

A long dead artist's eyes
and mine became the living

Eyes that saw the same
demeanor of a god.

DANGER DANCE

I know a place where wild Hemlock grows
Lush as parsley, edible to the eye,
It is a secret place to be
And wonder why Socrates

                              Chose sour tea.

Did he discuss the taste or just relate
The growing weight within his legs?

The curly Hemlock bends and bows,
Is a caress between my toes
As I crush its lethal fare
Beneath my steps
                          In summer air.

Shall I construe my danger dance
As joy within my weightless legs?

I know a field where the Hemlock knows
Abundancy, but there my thoughts
Are cautious counterfeits,
There I may dance, but fingers never must
                  Touch Hemlock lips.

PART TWO
Perspective

J. Cody

SNODGRASS SURVIVAL MANUALS

Starting each topic with a common truth
will command the respect of your audience.

        In the dark, with your flashlight and your gun
        find their startled eyes and then shoot quickly.

Standing enhances prestige forcing the other's
gaze upward; stay seated if you are short.

        The Fer-de-Lance will attack without warning;
        The cure for its venom may kill you.

A certain distinction in dress sets you apart
from inferiors and furthers prestige.

        Going unshod where barefooted natives
        drive pigs will give you hookworm.

Use your secretary to advantage
to block unwelcome callers and distractions.

        With heavy training you can survive
        the jungle with only a machete.

OLLEJ OF THE MYTHIC WARRIORS

There's a couple of yowling cats in Ollej.
They're chasing a one-eyed rat through Ollej.

He was wrapped in the crisis line,
declared disconnected, and

he was sent to the local E.R.
and had his wide surprised
orifices calmed into
narrow commas and his
confused ideology was ejected
and egresses through polyethylene
tubes along with Seconal pulp.

But they couldn't drain out the animals
without lowering the all-over pressure
and creating a permanent scar.
They gave him a prescription for Curare:
one dart, *q.i.d.* and as needed
(consult your physician if pain persists).

There were one thousand poems
engraved on the needle,
and a couple of cats
scratching in Ollej.

Kool, Kcid, Kool!
Kool on tops.

He was sent to the local
displaced psyche society
and had his Social Conscience
recollected and they told him
that there wasn't any social stigma
attached to a head transplant.

But they couldn't transplant the animals
as it would cause a head rejection and
constant infection of the civic duty.
They gave the rat an eye prosthesis
and sutured where indicated
(if fever persists five days or more
consult your S.P.C.A.).

A catheter is leaking
words into a bottle
and the poem is
pink drainage
on the cotton
in the wound.

O, O, O,
Look, Dick, look!
Look, no Spot.

There's a loud, loud growl in Ollej,
They've caught a glass-eyed rat in Ollej.

A MINOR DISTRACTION

Even the most
minor distraction
can disturb
a high point
of concentration
when the need
for a state
of finer mental
interaction
may concede
that the difference
between good and great

        (Phone is ringing)
              (Answered)
                  (Wrong number)
                    is total
application   and
                involvement.

THE STARMAKER

Someone climbed a lamppost in San Francisco
and holding the paintbrush in his teeth

Grasped the pole between his thighs
and pried the lid from a can of paint,

There might have been a prowl car cruising
or a few wary strollers could have stoned him,

But only some shadows waltzed behind windows
when he carefully layered the paint on the brush,

Softly stroking the lamp-globe black
and sealing the hot light in,

He practiced his craft with expertise
then scissored his cramped legs home.

Light jammed against the black partition,
reached nova force and clicked out the world.

BLUE BOY ON DARK BACKGROUND

after T. Gainsborough, 1727-1788

Street lights snap on the dark
a wait away.
Cold twilight calls
a laughing face
to hurry to his meal.

Blue-bruised
feet,
skip wildly.

Dusty naked tot-toes
smash down damp
brown butts
and plunks of spit.

Crusty knees and arms
above the skipping feet
child bird-mouth shrieks,

> "Crack and reds,
> The gang sez
> Your ma's in bed."

Careful not to stumble
on shattered pavement,
hurried legs piston home
sprint dervishly to the stoop,
pump three flights to his door.

Squat down and wait a bit.
Surveying with a glint
his panting dog
the human bird decides,

> "Mama's probably home,
> I heard the toilet flush."

THE NEON MODEL AND THE AD MAN

She is a lady
with a T.V. in her belly,
there's a new prescription
in the corner of her legs
and two big buttons
with a dot in the middle
dart from side to side
at the pull of a string,

a tape-recorded message
tells the time
from behind her parted
orthodontured teeth
she cups a chrome toaster
in each hand
and can pop a slice
of mother in your mouth.

He charms the ear
to smile and tell,
    The time is
             winding,
to tweak a cord
and bring the eyes
to moan,
a fevered call
and a quick
taste of mom
and his navel
grasps a channel
lines of flicks
chew a message
biting corners in a capsule
that leaves them asking,
    What are buttons for?

THE HEADHUNTER'S WIFE

He shouldn't have brought it home,
it's a foul trophy and on the shady
side of ethics to capture
an enemy's spirit. Yet
it is an ancient custom.

I'll pierce it with a stick and hold
the odor away with a few spice leaves
pushed in my nostrils.
I may as well not gamble with
an enemy spirit.

It's a painstaking chore to pick
it clean down to the browbone
and make the thing gleam correctly.
Boring the temple hole is a skill
my mother taught me.

This is the part that makes me back away,
I'd refuse to do it if it wasn't fresh,
flushing the gray soup out from the hole,
cautiously, it easily spills,
I've ruined it often.

He's a bit haughty, too impatient,
holding his dish that way, while
I heat it in the skullpan over a
slow fire, but I'll have it out of the
house when he eats it.

THE JUSTICE PROCLAMATION

He had a slate
when he was a child,
he bought it for a quarter
that he stole from his mother.

Blowing the chalk dust
clear of the slate,
he wrote over and over again,
I am a thief.

INSPECTION BY DAYLIGHT

The day is hanging around
until dinnertime
though I've cursed it,
yelled sour obscenities
and tried to heave
its bulk out of my way.

I'm an old blustering child
and I know I must wait
while the light
dawdles and probes
the sores on my face.

MEDICAL MUSIC

News Item: *In a medical miracle today, half a human being was amputated at the waist. The patient's recovery was uneventful.*

> If they do a
> hemicorporectomy
> to me, shall I have
> half a fancy funeral
> with hymns and flowers
> and weep with the mourners
>   who wheel me away?

FLYCASTING

To place this comma ","
correctly between
two wary words
requires an agile hand
with the pen
casting the inkline
until it stops
just here ","

and fools you
you think
catching poems
is well-schooled words
lurking in a cool place
luring us
to where the monster
swims in his Loch
so you and I
can net him
even though
both of us know
that catching poems
is questions "?"

PAST. FUTURE?

B.C.

All our poems were burned
in the Archives at Alexandria
when a few playful generals,
intrigued by the hot limbs
sprouting between their legs,
grew fields of flame
with a little spit
and a little flint.

A.D.

We write a million new poems
shape the ink into new questions,
grow thoughts on pages,
we laugh or rage
then slip our silent voices
into dusty library stacks
and wait for a Hydrogen flower
grown with a little switch
and a little spit.

Epilogue

We are billions of poems, humans
learning each day paths to travel
truths to follow, passing on
to each other, hopes, dreams
of the world in peaceful accord,
pleading for time to control
mushrooming death clouds,
with our struggles,
with our hearts.

WOMEN'S YEAR POEM

Listen to sounds from the heaving earth
birthing the newest music.

This is the sound of women's hearts
beating in unity.

This is the night of the rushing wind
pounding its way to freedom.

This is the time when the rising clouds
will blaze the sky with lightning.

Now is the time for women's voice
to rouse the world with reason.

This is the night when the bravest souls
will find the path to freedom.

DARK GLASSES

The sun raves
of its lavish
clarity
but my eyes
don't listen,

they keep seeing
the moon whisper
through
willow tree
fingers.

PART THREE
Lifeblood

Judith Cody

LOOKING UNDER FOOTPRINTS

Search the ground with heels,
Wedge curved toes into the moist root food
Until our arches slip into their precise cast,
Urge feet, firmly onto their earth pedestal
And touch gravity touching us,
Squeeze the world's grasp.

    The world is rolling underfoot, but not away from us,
    We are provided with the place where we will be created.

The world is holding on throughout its taut and ripened peel,
Down past the feedings in the longest tap roots
Drilled by the oldest Ponderosa pines
Until this heavy grip embraces mountain embryos,
Ocean nuclei, unerupted lava lakes,
Farther, bruising the stony unripe earth fruit,
The world's grasp is great enough to weld its molten pit.

    The world is rolling underfoot, but not away from us,
    We are provided with the place where we will be created.

Search the ground with hands, eyes,
Reach as far as human membrane can endure
Embrace the varied creatures whose existence creates
Patterns in the texture of our transparent world
Burrowed within this planet's atmosphere, seek
From that instant we uncurl from the mother flesh
And grow each of ourselves among all of ourselves.

    The world is rolling underfoot, but not away from us,
    We are provided with the place where we will be created.

Encapsulated in its unseen core unheard of shudders radiate
From this earth's inception,
We can only hear the pain-cry from the seeds
Enclosed within these human selves,
Though we share this same fertility with
The central seed at our true center
A thousand miles beneath our footsteps.

WHEN THE WIND FANS A SPIDER WEB

Seeing with his feet
the world's vibrations,
his arachnid tendency
to flee
is canceled
by his passion
for a fly.

SAY IT

Begin simply
say,
    I love you.

O
do not
be
ornate
but
declare,
    I do love you.

Try
to convey
its
weight
its
sedative way
and

Proclaim,
    I do most definitely love you.

Calmly
state it,
> *I love you, I love, love, love you.*

O
you
may learn
to believe it.

A SMILE

opened
your face
wide enough
so that
I saw
the food
on your tongue.

        The Eye

in your throat
smiles
at you
observing
your teeth talk.

TOPICS OVER TEA
. . . philosophy student

Here my Love, may I pour you tea?
The steaming amber liquids gurgling flow
Alerts the silence of the room,
And captures in its mirror depths
My gesture meant to speak a word.

The sweet-tossed glances of our eyes
Meet above the cooling cups of tea,
And disregard our state of being,
Finite, pink-shelled human beings
Who die a little every breath.

Will we create our compromise
And loving think just of our days
Softly curled around the nights?

Here we are, You and I,
Spawned in reckless heat.
Long-shot sperm lashing in ahead
One night when two others coupled
At the proper moment.
What odds!
A neurotic gambler's life's delight.
Happy Birthday, Bright Eyes.
Your last
Will be a sure thing, unlike the first.

You and I, here we are,
Expanding Universe?
Well, do you accept the theory?
Does it expand as a bubble,
And burst?
Will all the gooey segments of the ruptured wreck
Fly hither, thither, where, and splat?
On what?

Give me a sign, Oh, Omen of the Ages.
There!
Swirled in soaring arcs before my startled eyes
A dove of milken white and holy wing.
This pure white bird chose to fly
Through this monoxide mist to signal me!
The holy bird directly seeks for me
And hovers comfort by my side.
Must be the sign . . .
The green-tinged muck he left upon my sleeve.

You and I,
Tears transcended from primordial seas
Weeping our tears which migrate to the skies
To rain upon a bramble
Sprung from a soldier's grave
Weeping tears to rust the lustrous steel
Incasing flaming journeys into space.

Where are we?
Are we in a china tea cup
Drifting on the corpses of those who went ahead?
Cities of stenched hides beneath their coffin lids,
Once held smiles across their rotting mouths.

This moment over tea is ours,
The next, the worms that feed the doves,
Frugally, our flesh will be dispersed
Among the many hungry jaws of earth
To be consumed indifferently.

Even the ripples we have bent
Through time and space will be erased,
Yet, leave the echo of a kiss.

We beings create our sheltered place
And seek in its elusive shade
A sentry for our cleft in space
To guard the china god we've made.

ONCE UPON A TIME THE MARBLE STATUE BECAME A REAL LIVE MAN

"Wizened balls crouch between my thighs,
they are threaded with a few new hairs
proclaiming an archeological wonder,
a squat Cro-Magnon artifact,
restored to reveal the linework
and displayed under
a fluorescent unveiling
in a free-form pseudo-futuristic
Museum of Antiquity.

What if there's a third one
still stuck in my belly?"

ENCOUNTER

1

We met for lunch.

It was

        a platter of flowers
        a bottle of red mountain
        and a dusty sheet.

It was

        petals stuck to my back
        pink stains on the curtains
        a roomful of flowing skin and

our own unlocking of the night
at noon.

Soft breathing stuffed the room
with smiling moons.

       You were
            a felled ponderosa
       and I caressed
            a fragrant platter.

2

Their faceless sun
slapped across my eyes
an aberration of the lens
that crisply caught details
in the creases
of their lips.

ODONATA

Dragonflies *in copula*
level off in shade,
a fluid spectrum enclasped
by Permian biplanes.

SAVE THE VISIONS

Catch the moon
In a dixie cup,
Chill your crusted thirst
With the big night eye
Peering at sun flares
Through a cataract,
But the moon has darkness
To view visions by,
Then is the time,
Sneak a few cool drams
Set aside for the scalding years
Between dreams.

LOVING POEM

My womb is an orchid
languishing in darkness.

She flares her purple petals
to cup the warm rain
and sway on the stalk.

My womb is a jaguar
lurking in darkness.

She fans her nimble talons
to catch the night prey
drawn to her red mouth.

My womb is a dancer
loving in darkness.

She flicks her supple torso
to dip, to glide, to rise,
above restraint upon your stage.

PLATO'S HERMAPHRODITE

They is a comely being
and they breasts
swing in soft harmony,
swallows nests
of intricate construction,
nipples bob
in erectile seduction
above the swell
of pectoral brawn
they duplicity is dawn
and dusk,
the black and the white
swan.

They grips the ruddy fruits
of virile fox
in the vixen's bifurcation,
the interlocks
conjugate ally and foe
in solemn
amazement as a low
shaman's moan
dispels a startled smile
there is pain to reconcile
with joy
when form is born flesh
-wild.

LOVERS AND OTHER SPIES

You have keen ears
you can hear me
slip through the dark.

You listen, listen
O,
you listen
for my whisper-moans,
for my loud red rhythms
twisting past the darkness.

You listen
for my cries.

I am quiet,
I listen.

UNMENTIONED

Anoplura,
clutching a chitin tree
in the moist tropic of Mons.

There, on a secret knoll
in a perpetual shade
he is plumped in the shadows.

Littlest vampire,
never to see the sun.

Phthirus pubis,
frailest unpublic flake,
afraid of a face.

THE ALISON RAINBOW SONG

Who is it? What is it breathing up ahead
filling silence with anxious rasps rolling
in stagnant steam in the distant cold,
yet close enough for chills to streak my shoulders,
in the distance I can see *What*
as a dim reflection of my past.

Once as bright as all the brilliant fruits I ate
and as warm as the flesh I embraced,
for I suppose I'd loved that young girl,
she was I, or did I only love
her sturdy arms and legs moving boundaries,
walking through the mountains, cities, and skies,
or was it her big greedy eyes stealing faces for me,
bringing me joy in the whirling parade of things.
Was it her womb I prided my young self on?
Young girls believe they can replace themselves.

O how helpless we are without bodies to store us,
the vapor we are is so thin
it drifts but an instant between life and dying
evading the heat of the sun that could dry it
as it tries to escape processional heart beats
marching it forward and down.

I looked at the Foreword and chose not to see,
the choice was a vaporous curse
trailing alongside my legs as they tightened
to spring into loosening steps
each fainter than the last sound they made
and never as loud again.

Following eyes I feared, for their vision,
my mind watched the body teased on by the monster,
defiant, I sang in that unwilled finale,

> "Come on all you boys
> who have been where I'm going!
> Come on all you girls who know!
> Won't you tell me
> if I'll be returning from there
> and why I have to go?"

A song is a stone human vapor can throw
with vengeance and joy at the lips which reveal it
while slowly exhaling the self to extinction
along with the soul, creeping, pleading,
forced by its fragile condition to follow.

Up ahead grew bright in the way of an eye,
searching your own
for something to quell the craving that lights it.

My patient companion dimmed
when I eagerly displayed *Paradise Lost,*
King Lear and *The Holy Bible*;
dimmer yet when I waved *Dante's Inferno*
in my left hand and *The Iliad* in my right.
It harshly inhaled light, then exhaled darkness
at my playing of Brahms and Beethoven.

Struck blind, I threw the books aside,
the music stopped and once again I saw the breather's shadow
that would not feed on these great human thoughts
yet halted without luster while I offered
my shiny beads, silk sashes, both shoes
then angrily tossed off my yellow dress.

Again it reached its turgid form for me;
now I felt its heavy breath
as I rushed to find its nourishment
so, naked, threw myself supine upon my life's discards
and waited for the thing to mount
for even that must end
to leave me with my body self
containing only me.

Rage could name the sound it made,
lust or joy were not the food it ate,
nor did it mount or care to learn.

A song is a stone human vapor can throw
matching the warrior mist of the soul
striding within the body of me
singing an arrogant tune,

> "Come on all you boys!
> Come on all you girls!
> You who have been to this place before,
> Won't you tell me
> if I'll be returning from here?
> I'll build you a shrine with an emerald door."

O how helpless we are without bodies to store us,
the wonder we are is so fine
it seeps through our pores
with the sweat, with the terror
dissolving raw bones, digesting our joy
and grinding the stew through our bowels.

Pure memory poked me from my fear-stench,
and sketched the face of Faustus and Mephistopheles
whispering what the loud evil wanted
was the usual soul exchange.
Run blood! Drip my soul
onto some contract this panting glow demands
I shall salvage what scraps of me it leaves
and shield myself a little longer,
perhaps to steal it back.

It shrieked. A cough like a laugh
caught me in its fumes,
what naked me was left to give
I bent my head to weigh,
then knew what would be taken,
I saw through waves of body heat
that I was also only
lean carnivore's meat!

Meat of elephants and whales,
meat of men and women
was fulfillment for the breathless hunger
pausing to dissolve our body cases.

I saw the panting glow at last,
saw the universal cretin
which only accidentally swallows souls.

        "Come on all you boys!
        Come on all you girls!
        I can tell you how to get here
        but you never need to know."

PART FOUR
Soul Tears

Judith Caly

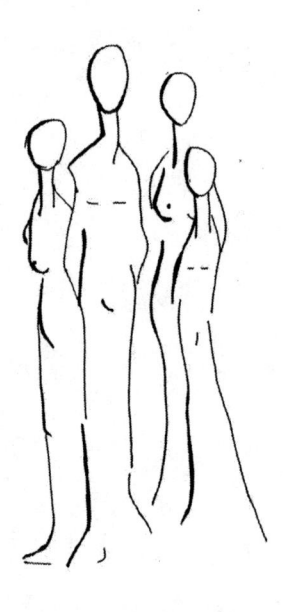

THE FOREVER DIORAMA

*What startling thing did Ethan Brand
see in the diorama? "I find it to be
a heavy matter in my shadow box,"
said the Jew of Nuremburg.*-Hawthorne

Summer advances a few meters each year
raw earth and life pods
staining the glacial plough
are passing the frosted window,
through the wavy ice-sheet
I can see the sun bursting trees,
stinging the earth into a blur of flora,
certain smudges separate,
I see they are animate
as speck by speck
the mural crawls.

Form against form
adheres and recoils
stretched to the nexus
infusing the heat of mitosis
through a finite millions
indifferently melting the frozen eons.

The white of past eternities
cools the eye-gel and tints
the rage of green fertility
a distant event;
this is the ice age of our minds,
a thick fusing of the spectrum
into an impenetrable arctic horizon.

Endless thoughts in endless nights
light the holiness of black
and silhouette the soul
gnawing at its mouth,
poetry wails without words
minor variations of the moon communion,
when even the devil is gentle.

WHO KILLED THE VULTURE WHILE HE WAITED FOR THE BEACHED WHALE TO DIE?

The vulture is strung on a stone
sticky with blood
from the wound in his breast.

He waited and wanted
to eat death by the throatfuls
to plunge to the liver of the whale
then slick with the grease of feasting,
he'd glide in the thick urgent sky of it.

The bird would have waited,
patiently waited,
for the whale's last heavy thrashes
gouging glyphs in the sand,
and then he'd have watched
the lenses grow cloudy
before he peeled them away.

THE PRINTER

Yesterday is a
smeared typographical
error I'm not able to
read without a
laughable attempt to
see what it really said.

CHILD OF THE VIRGINS

Black hems dragging the dust
into footprintless trails
aren't covering legs,
but in the wilted darkness
ebbitts hold tall faces
searching high above my head.

O clever child!
To shake the hair
into a berry bush
before my eyes
and angling through the stems
I steal a view
of the nun's procession.

Through the stations,
the decades of Mary
(pretty like my older cousin)
paced by the father's voice
ten commandments
roll like crooked boulders
into the catacombs
veining the thoughts of my eyes.

Wind presses the veils
into similar folds
over the hundred eyes
that see me as a dark
hairy bush on the edge
of a holy parade,
> *When is the lady coming?*

Wind rattles the crosses.

I whisper in a pure
seizure of craving,
> *When is the lady coming*
> *with her mother's smile*
> *and up turned palms*
> *and child-toed feet*
> *poking from silk*
> *and stepping on snakes?*

Shush! Black veils are wagging
and shushing at me
as they tread by on ebbitts
more able than legs,
more holy than feet,
leaving no footprints,
leaving no sound,
only a back and forth indistinct swoosh.

The lady is coming
on a thick platform,
stooping the last nuns
close to the ground,
their long beads are clinking
over the roadway
they never look up
to see her pink smile,
chipped in the sunlight,
smiling at flowers
wired to her hands.

THE EXHUMATION

He is saying,

      "You have a few months."

It's hurting my face
to keep it from messing
this pristine room.

And I am five years old
getting lost in legs on buses,
thinking the newspaper
is to keep the rain
from the crack under the door.
I'll never dare
to grow as big as mother,
(the pink sweaty monster).

He is telling this kid about
rads and bombardment
and that they might banish
the massed invasion
bursting the cells.

Holding the X-ray up to the light
the sun silhouettes the smokey profile
leering inside myself.

And I'm three years old
with licorice in my hair,
burying my goldfish
under a brick in the yard,
and digging him up,
with a teaspoon,
one week later.

AKHENATON'S HYMN TO ATON

Isis, moonbearer, flame of Osiris,
I have stolen her eyes from stone and
Gouged the whore's face from our walls,
Ra burns, Amon Ra turns from the sun
A drift of cinders settling in sand.

Aton! I have split the altars of Amon's spawn
And you are now the god, the thousand hands
Enclosing my man's form from dreams of Set
Whose priests are preaching murder in our streets.
Aton! "Make not my glad cause cause of mourning."

Aton! I have crushed false gods for you,
Light the sun again for me
As bright as all the worlds
That were entwined
In my first thought of you.

NO REFUNDS, NO EXCHANGES

Snugly, you've sewn my skin.

Make it looser in the middle.

The seams are brittle stitches
they will snap when I breathe,

Strands are snagging on the walls
and the blood beads like dew

While I sponge away the drops
more are oozing from the holes,

Red, red sweat wells from
the patterns traced on me
by needle pricks.

STILLBIRTHS

There's been a strange revision
at the *Brain Cutting Sessions.*

They're cutting fresh wild flowers
instead of cutting children.

Violet, baby girl,
        " Brain discarded."

Goldenrod, baby boy,
        " Brain recommended."

Water lily child
the Buddha smile was
slit from your face on schedule

And the petals slid soundlessly
bright moist roses
on the cutting room floor.

Wild field flowers
your budding feet will never
walk on the sunlit earth

Now a thousand watts of tungsten light
bare your narrow bones.

Windsown children
pinched from the earth

You are the flowers
born for the cutters.

BIOLOGICAL WAR NEEDLES

Knitting,
it surpasses death,
it is bloated, purple death
bursting at the joints
yet still I curl,
I twist and draw
the wool between my hands.

Pakistan goats,
dead from anthrax,
had their fur
spun into skeins,
their wool
makes mittens.

A man
who loved his wool too much
deftly twirled his yarn
too many times
too many lovely colors
delighted him,
he died
from knitting mittens.

ELEGY

for Grandfather, after Dylan Thomas

O the rage whoring within me!
The imbecile fury that could thrust
my hands into your gravetop
and scrape it back until my arms
burned in the sockets, until the raw
pulse of my fingers left my own warmth,
my own life in that cold place!

THE OFFERING

Each day
>I am getting harder to carry,

Teeth worn
>close to the gums are losing their hold,
>the heavy sack of me is spilling

Thick gourds,
>turnips and a few worm thinned grapes,

Overripe,
>making it awkward to walk on the

Slick phlegm.

Backward,
>with my one pitted eye, I see the

Snail's trail
>Marking its way for decades to the

Storehouse,

Forward,
>with my ten dragging roots, there waits the
>earth-struck throat
>moist with hunger.

THE TEAR GOD

*The Chinese saved tears
in vials as sacred
gifts of spent sorrow.*

The tears are livid stains
disguising her face,
a swollen effigy

Of the tear god's ghost, whose
tribute evaporates
unrecorded.

The idol grins at the
great blubbering doll's
liquid incense; preens

Before her vulgar in-
tonations; winks and
dozes through vespers.

*In the skull's cloister
of the tear god
grief is anonymous.*

WOMAN LEFT ON A DESERT PLATEAU

Stiff brown stalks
poke from split clay
and crumble
in the sun's trembling heat
(it thins the air cracking
through my lips).

The stale plateau
is wavering
and breaking in the light,
pieces chip my eyes
and crease my throat.

A dying fly
probes a globe of sweat
suspended in an arm hair,
his wide eye facets
(dull with dust)
accept four thousand
acid fragments
formed in a last
mosaic of me.

THE BLANKET

1
Inca Women were once honored
as the great weavers,
carders, combers, spinners of wools
flying fingers deftly flicked,
twisted strands faster than
the eye of man could keep track of
wonder at.

2
While another woman in a far,
quiet secret place wove a blanket
from her wools
cut from sheeps backs and bellies
some from the thick
winter coats of horses,
of dogs, of goats,
even the young long hairs of special men,
loved most specially.

And the woman wound her daughter's
long dark hairs
curled them deep
inside the great thick blanket,
and colors of many creatures
spun, twined and whirled
within the blanket
like in the meadow
after the thundering spring rain
after the curtain of grey clouds
rushed away opened
revealing the hue bowed rain
beneath the rolling sun lights.

3
Evilly cold
bitter winds biting the flesh
someone lost somewhere
beyond all shelter.
Death squats on the path
home is too far to find
to live that long trek

there is no confessional
from the devil snow
white demon swirls prettily
coy alluring to the cold drowsy
sleep forever
ah o rest no do not.

4
The woman wandered
swathed in her blanket
of many colored creatures
reaching the white mountain top
two days and a moonless night distant
from her home fire,

a naked man reared,
came from behind the pines
where he had hid himself
from the wind, the curious same wind
that battled his fire sticks
made it impossible to create the art,
the fire.

Around his waist on a
thick strap hung a heavy
flint knife flecked with dark blood,
hair and beard were white
with frost
he seemed to have the look
of an old, wise man,
he was neither
she could see that at once.

And he saw the great
blanket with the woman
drawn all inside
warm and peering out through
the small open face fold
where her breath left gentle
puffs before her careful steps.

5
It was as if a meadow full
of bright birds had that moment
appeared from some shaman's
pipe right there on the
horizon to horizon vista
where the tender
snow entombed summits.
He laughed
the sudden waves
of bright sound
causing tiny avalanches
on the pine tree tips,
the beauty the wonder
of the woman with the blanket.

WINGS OF GLORY

Why fly on unfurled wings frugally cast
Of gloomy charms in sculpture's clay,
But fly on wayward to the last
Of one sun shocked and cleaved day,
Then glean a laughing moment's haughty breath
To whip a breeze and tip a wing to death.

WRAPPING GIFTS

You wrapped xmas gifts
your hands moving in
amazing, intricate patterns
controlling the brilliant papers
sparkling ribbons tinseled
curvaceous bows twining, turning
in confined choreography
released from your
engineer's finger tips,

Here-there paper creased in perfect
line taped-squared, aligned, magical
engineering principles
embodied in the age-old precision
of human hands flowing
in the beauty of loving work.

CALIFORNIA DROUGHT MAKES TV WINTER NEWS

Hummingbirds perched
in a shelter saved

peeking at the TV camera

What's a hummer to do?

Starve . . . iridescent coma . . . fall
  and
wait   on
   the   frozen

     ground.

Tiny brilliant bird toy
red-crayon-tip-size
heart, throbbing
hundreds of throbs
in sixty seconds
can only stay awake
maybe fifteen minutes
with no nectar.

No water.... no flowers... no nectar...
no bugs
   ... no warmth left
anywhere to go at night.

Three years without
rain killed most flowers the
tough survivors didn't last
in two weeks of twenty
degree frost freeze out.

Last living plants
all dead brown, brittle,

food gone

   cold death coming

      fast.

THREE TRUE WOLVES

I would keep three true wolves
they would not be the wolves
of ecological wonderland
wolves conversing with caribou
wolves adept at signals
wolves toiling for dinner on the tundra.

No.

They would be real wolves
created by real thoughts and dreams
put to form from eons of fantasy
fleshed through and through
with real nightmare muscle.

What wolves!
Teeth
muzzles
ears
legs uncontrollable
carnivorous abandon
terrifying beyond all reason

Snarl alone entering the human ear
would cause instant ejection of all fluids.

Three real wolves
wild and free
as imagination, as yesterday.

PART FIVE
Epilogue

NOTES AND THOUGHTS ON THE POEMS

Ars Longa Vita Brevis:
Art is long, life is short. Indeed.

Biological War Needles:
Yes, it's true. The man lived in a far off country, but died from the disease. Things seem to move very fast in this new world we've made.

The Blanket:
In the 1990's a man was found partly thawed on a high glacier in Europe. He had fire and hunting tools with him; he had never come home with his game thousands of years ago. The "iceman's" photo was all over the media. His story struck everyone, and me. I wondered if only the woman who had once loved, a man like him, had managed to go to a similar mountain somewhere in the world of time where so many had been lost. I wondered and I knew it must have happened many times.

Encounter:
A moment of perfect love is an eternity of dreams.

The Offering:
Ultimate biodegradability. Free.

Ollej of the Mythic Warriors:
Curare is a brilliant invention by African Pygmies; made from plants and put on darts it paralyzed prey. Today, it is used for certain medical reasons, found in Encarta. O! Ollej is not a Viking, except in striving. His timeline is contemporary American overcontrolled, and the consequence can be seen backwards.

Once Upon a Time the Marble Statue Became a Real Live Man:
Don't you think that there must have been a million dreamers, wishing that Michelanglo Buonarroti's glorious stone David would live? Like Pinocchio?

Plato's Hermaphrodite:
He believed that in the beginning of time, male and female humans existed as a single entity. While trying hard to imagine such a construction, this poem was done. A divorce, of some ancient sort, cut the being apart; the result is evident today.

Say It:
There are times when it is way too hard to say these words. Practice; rehearse.

Stillbirths:
Brain Cutting Session is a teaching session for physicians to learn what killed the new, sweet babies who are born dead. The official entry on the final schedule may read "brain discarded," meaning the brain is "normal" so there is no need for further analysis. If the entry says, "brain recommended," this means that abnormal neurological findings will require more study. I accidentally stumbled onto such a "schedule" while in a hospital for my own illness. It was a sudden painful glimpse

of extreme reality that I could never forget. I could only light a candle for the tiny dead.

Snodgrass Survival Manuals:

A kind of real time adaptation of two manuals of proper comportment. One was a book of rules for those who would become CEOs; while the other manual was a military survival handbook for the soldier in the tropics. Oddly identical.

Unmentioned:

Anoplura, is the third sub-order, the Sucking Lice. *Phthirus pubis,* is the embarrassing, Crab louse. A king in its own world.

Watching for Tlaloc to Cool the Sun:

Tlaloc, the ancient rain god, found in Mexico, is also known as *Chac* to the Mayas, and *Cocijo* to the Zapotecs in Mesoamerican mythology. *Tezcatlipoca* stole *Xochiquetzal,* goddess of flowers and love, from Tlaloc. In our time, the massive stone sculpture of *Tlaloc* was brought from its archeological site, then paraded through the streets of Mexico City to be displayed in the beautiful new museum. People lined the streets to see the exhumed old god; it rained on them. There had been a drought.

DEDICATIONS

Ars Longa Vita Brevis to Pablo and Leo
Child of the Virgins to Nan
Entering the Singing Place to the Biospherans, John, Laser, Tango and Gaie
Flycasting to my brothers-in-law and <u>all</u> my nephews
The Forever Diorama to Rob
A Minor Distraction to Barry
Looking Under Footprints to Michael
Save the Visions to Trish
Topics Over Tea in memory of my mother and father
Watching for Tlaloc to Cool the Sun to Hector and Susanna
Wings of Glory to Guy
Woman Magic to my sisters, sisters-in-law, and <u>all</u> my nieces
Wrapping Gifts to my husband (as is this book)
Moth in the Footlights in memory of my grandparents
Dark Glasses to Nelly